British
WILDFLOWERS
& TREES

First published in 2013 by Miles Kelly Publishing Ltd
Harding's Barn, Bardfield End Green, Thaxted, Essex, CM6 3PX, UK

Copyright © Miles Kelly Publishing Ltd 2013

This edition printed in 2016

4 6 8 10 9 7 5

Publishing Director *Belinda Gallagher*
Creative Director *Jo Cowan*
Editorial Director *Rosie Neave*
Editors *Carly Blake, Claire Philip*
Designers *Jo Cowan, Carmen Johnson, Rob Hale*
Cover Design *Jo Cowan*
Image Manager *Liberty Newton*
Production *Elizabeth Collins, Caroline Kelly*
Reprographics *Stephan Davis, Thom Allaway, Jennifer Cozens*
Woodland Trust Advisor *Graham Blight*
The Wildlife Trusts Advisor *Adam Cormack, Mary Porter*
Assets *Lorraine King*

Miles Kelly would like to thank **The Wildlife Trusts** and **The Woodland Trust** for their valuable contributions to this book.

ISBN 978-1-78209-129-5

Printed in China

British Library Cataloguing-in-Publication Data
A catalogue record for this book is available from the British Library

ACKNOWLEDGEMENTS

The publishers would like to thank the following artists who have contributed to this book:
Bridgette James, Mike Foster, Andrea Morandi, Mike Saunders, Vivien Wilson

The publishers would like to thank the following sources for the use of their photographs:

Colin Varndell 19(r), 25(r), 35(r), 37(r), 39(r), 43(r), 73(r), 79(r), 87(r), 91(r) & 95(r)
Dennis McGuire 123(tl) **Dreamstime.com** 126 Elena Elisseeva; 146 Griffin024; 164 Ivonnewierink;
192 Pavel Kalouš; 212 Ryszard; 220 Marcoregalia **FLPA** 22 B. Borrell Casals; 26 Nigel Cattline; 38 Tony Hamblin;
48 G E Hyde; 60 Tony Wharton; 62 Tony Hamblin; 66 Richard Becker; 70 & 72 Robert Canis; 73(c) Roger Wilmshurst;
78 Tony Wharton; 82 Gary K Smith; 90 Roger Wilmshurst; 92 Richard Becker; 94 Martin B Withers; 98 John Hawkins;
100 Nigel Cattlin; 104 Martin Woike/Foto Natura; 108 Joke Stuurman-Huiteman/Foto Natura/Minden Pictures;
110 John Hawkins; 112 Robert Canis; 134 FotoNatura/FN/Minden; 136 Tony Wharton; 144 Richard Becker;
172 Erica Olsen; 184 Martin H Smith; 190 Peter Entwistle; 198 Tony Wharton; 210 Gary K Smith; 216 Tony Hamblin;
222 Bob Gibbons **Fotolia.com** 18 Gail Johnson; 19(c) AndreyTTL; 34 Bill; 51(c) Robyn Mackenzie;
83(c) Olena Kucherenko; 122(tr) Elenathewise, (br) Steve Smith; 124 Freddy Smeets;160 Jgz; 174 Oleg Belyakov;
200 Eric Weight; 218 Martina Berg **Jo Brewer** 156 & 176 **Mike Alsford** 10 **NHPA** 16 Martin Garwood;
36 Stephen Dalton; 140 Dr Eckart Pott; 180 Stephen Dalton **Philip Wells** 158 **Photolibrary.com** 30 Harold Taylor
Shutterstock.com Cover Valentyn Volkov; 1 Madlen; 3 Regien Paassen; 6–7 Ivan M Munoz; 116–117 Oleg Belyakov;
40 Grant Glendinning; 44 stoupa; 106 Cristian Mihai; 120 leonid_tit; 130 MarkMirror; 138 Douglas Freer; 186 Olga
Nikonova **Still Pictures** 59(r) D.Harms/WILDLIFE **The Wildlife Trusts** 142 Rachel Scopes; 132 Neil Aldridge; 148, 150,
162 & 170 Les Binns; 178 & 182 Philip Precey; 188 Eddie Asbery; 204 Dave Appleton; 214 Adam Cormack
WTPL 12, 13(l), (r); 15 **WTPL/Pete Holmes** 11(tl, ctr, cbl, br)

All other images from the Miles Kelly Archive

Every effort has been made to acknowledge the source and copyright
holder of each picture. Miles Kelly Publishing apologises for any
unintentional errors or omissions.

Made with paper from a sustainable forest

www.mileskelly.net   info@mileskelly.net

WOODLAND
TRUST

THE wildlife TRUSTS

British
WILDFLOWERS
& TREES

Written by:

Camilla de la Bedoyère

Miles
Kelly

Contents

WILDFLOWERS

Checklist: Mark off your tree and wildflower sightings in the tick boxes.

TREES

Introducing Trees

We owe a lot to trees. They warm us, shelter us and provide us with building materials. If it wasn't for trees, this book wouldn't be printed on paper and you wouldn't be reading it!

The least we can do in return is get to know their names. Knowing what tree you are leaning against or standing under will give you an amazing insight into what's going on all around you. Being able to identify a tree means you can have a good guess at what species of butterfly and moth caterpillars may be chewing through its leaves, which birds may be nesting in its boughs and what fungi might burst through the leaf litter come the autumn.

But where to start? Well – you have already made the first step in tree identification by holding this book! Here, there are fifty fantastic tree species to discover, including those you may already recognise.

In this section you will find each species clearly presented. Use the images of the leaf, twig and tree shape to help with identification. Find essential information in the factfile, and use the photofile to discover what wildlife you might see living in or near the tree. Make sure to take notes and record your sightings and activities.

Most importantly, enjoy learning about these fascinating and important plants!

Nick Baker

Seasonwatch

Get up close to nature all year round with the Woodland Trust's nature detectives CLUB. Each season brings plenty of changes and events, from spring bluebells to juicy summer blackberries.

Spring: Look out for signs of the natural world bursting into life – discover blossoms on trees and hedges, identify new leaves emerging from buds and hunt for minibeasts.

explore a bluebell wood in spring

discover wildflowers in summer

Summer: Make the most of the year's longest days – have a picnic in the shade of a tree in full leaf, identify butterflies collecting nectar from flowers, sail a leaf boat down a stream, and capture a colourful wildflower meadow on camera.

play conkers in autumn

Autumn: Enjoy nature's dazzling autumn display – scrunch through colourful, fallen leaves, collect juicy blackberries to turn into tasty treats, plant an acorn and make a house for a hedgehog to hibernate in.

plant a tree in winter

Winter: Wrap up warm in these colder months and splash through puddles on a welly wander in the woods. You can also make a bird feeder and identify animal prints in the snow or mud.

Woodland Trust
**naturedetectives
CLUB**

Join the Woodland Trust's nature detectives CLUB to enjoy year-round family fun outdoors, with ideas and activities every week to make the most of each season. Club members get a fantastic wall chart with stickers and seasonal packs.

www.naturedetectives.org.uk/365

Wonderful woodlands

www.VisitWoods.org.uk

*I*f you like nature and outdoor adventures, the Woodland Trust's website VisitWoods.org.uk is a great place to discover amazing woodlands close to home, and all over the country.

Plan your visit

You can find your nearest wood with a simple postcode or town name search. There are over 10,000 woods on the database, so there's plenty to choose from.

Get exploring

VisitWoods.org.uk are always coming up with loads of new ideas for things to do in the woods. On the website you can download stuff to help you spot wildlife, go on a woodland scavenger hunt, build a cool den and even create your own tree sculpture.

Take part

The website is interactive, meaning you can share your wildlife sightings by uploading photos and recording your stories to document your adventures.

Log on today to start your woodland adventure!

WOODLAND TRUST

VisitWoods.org.uk

How to measure trees

Here are two easy, fun and safe ways to measures trees. For species that can live to an ancient age, measure the girth of the trunk. For species that are more short-lived, you can try measuring the height instead.

Once you have taken your measurements, remember to tick the 'Measured it!' stamp.

Measure the girth

If you have one, take a measuring tape, but if you don't, you can estimate the girth of the tree by hugging it!

Measuring tape Measure around the trunk at 1.5 metres from the ground. If you can't measure the tree at this height then make a note of the height at which you measured the girth.

Hugging A standard British hug (fingertip to fingertip) is 1.5 m long. With some friends, wrap your arms around the trunk so that your fingertips touch each others' fingertips. Each person around the tree equals one 'hug'.

If you can, work out exactly where the tree is on a map. Take some photos of the tree.

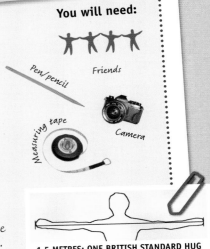

You will need:

Pen/pencil   Friends

Measuring tape   Camera

1.5 METRES: ONE BRITISH STANDARD HUG

Measure the height

1 Ask a friend to stand next to the tree.

2 Facing the tree, hold your ruler upright and at arms length. Walk away from the tree until it 'fits' on the ruler.

3 According to the ruler, record how tall your friend is and how tall the tree is. Work out how many times your friend goes into the height of the tree.

4 Multiply this number by your friend's actual height (in metres) and this will give you the rough height of the tree.

You will need:

30 cm ruler   Pen/pencil   A friend

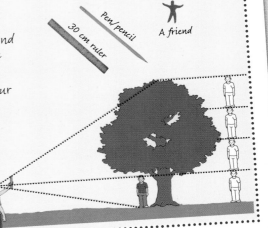

How to plant a tree

Planting trees is great for the environment and easier than you might think. Choose a native tree and the benefits are even greater as these provide food and shelter for our wildlife.

Planting your tree from a seed

Try planting a tree from seeds you have collected yourself. You can collect seeds from late summer to autumn, once they have started dropping from trees.

Collecting and preparing

Cones Let cones dry out naturally and they will release their seeds.

Fleshy fruits Remove all flesh from seeds, such as cherries, berries and apples, and put in water. Only use the seeds that sink.

 Nuts De-shell nuts, such as acorns and conkers, and put in water. Keep the nuts that sink.

Winged seeds Break in half to separate pairs. These can be planted with wings on.

Planting

1 All of the these seeds can be planted immediately in a container. Use small plant pots, old milk cartons or yogurt pots. Make holes in the bottom for drainage.

2 Fill containers with a mix of peat-free compost and sand. Sow alder, birch or pine seeds on top then cover with a thin layer of compost. Acorns and nuts should be sown about 5 cm deep. Press down the compost.

TOP TREE-PLANTING TIPS

○ If you have a small garden, avoid willow and poplar. Try hawthorn, hazel, holly, rowan, crab apple or box.

○ If you have a large, spacious garden, try oak, ash, beech, Scots pine or yew.

○ Make sure there is enough room for your tree to grow — don't plant it too close to buildings or pipes.

○ If you are planting more than one tree, leave 2 m between them.

3 You can leave the pots outside over autumn and winter. Put them in a shady spot against a wall and cover with mesh to protect from birds and mice.

4 Once your seeds have germinated in spring, keep them well watered. When your seedlings are 20 to 40 cm tall they are ready to plant out (see next page for details).

Planting your tree from a sapling

An easy way to plant a tree is from a sapling (partly grown tree). You can buy saplings from your local garden centre, or online at www.woodlandtrustshop.com/trees

1 Give the roots of your sapling a good soak in a bucket of water before you plant them.

2 Carefully remove the sapling from its container. Check it for damage and remove any broken roots.

3 Decide on your planting spot. Dig a hole twice as wide and slightly deeper than the sapling roots. Save the turf for later.

4 You may need to make the hole bigger to avoid bending the roots – try your sapling in the hole to check.

5 Place your sapling upright in the hole. Break up the dug-out soil and fill in carefully but firmly around the roots.

6 Tread down the soil firmly and add some more soil if needed. Tread down again.

7 Take the pieces of turf saved from earlier and place them upside down around your sapling and press them down.

8 Finally, 'heel in' the earth around the tree. Give your sapling a gentle tug – it should be firmly in place.

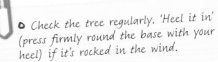

9 Tidy up and apply mulch (material laid down to keep in moisture) around the base of your sapling.

10 Start your tree diary by writing regular notes on your tree's progress.

LOOKING AFTER YOUR TREE

Now that you have planted your tree, you need to look after it:

◦ Keep a one-metre circle around the base free from grass and plants for the first year.

◦ Add some mulch around the base. Bark mulch is best, but newspaper or grass clippings are better than nothing! Mulch provides nutrients to the tree and keeps in moisture.

◦ Check the tree regularly. 'Heel it in' (press firmly round the base with your heel) if it's rocked in the wind.

◦ Small trees planted in the winter shouldn't need watering, but larger trees may need watering through the first year and during dry spells.

For more information visit:
www.woodlandtrust.org.uk/communitytrees

How to use

Use this guide to help you find your way around the tree section. Read information about 50 different species of trees, including vital statistics, wildlife you might see near the tree, detailed illustrations and simple identification tips.

Photofile
If you spot the bug, bird or fungus featured for each tree, tick the 'Seen it!' stamp.

My notes
Make notes about your tree sightings.

Measure
If you measure the girth or the height of the tree tick the 'Measured it!' stamp.

My drawings and photos
Fill these spaces with your sketches and photographs, and stick in a leaf or photo of the tree.

Identifying a tree

1 Look at the leaf... What basic leaf shape do you think it is – oval, long, hand-shaped, compound or needle?

2 Trees with similar leaf shapes are grouped together. The shape is shown in the top right of species.

3 Use the other illustrations to help you to confirm your identification.

MY OBSERVATIONS

Season:

Where is the tree?

Describe the tree:

What wildlife can you see?

How tall is your tree?

MY DRAWINGS AND PHOTOS

The striking hornet moth is rare in the UK. Adult moths lay their eggs in poplar trees, including black poplar. The larvae hatch and burrow into the wood, developing into adults in June and July.

SEEN IT?

MEASURED IT?

On my tree I saw: leaves ○ buds ○ fruit ○ flowers ○

22

14

Main text
Every right-hand page introduces you to a species.

Tree shape
Refer to the tree shapes to help identify the tree at different times of the year.

Leaf shape
Flick through the book to find the correct leaf shape section. Each section is colour coded for easy navigation.

Champion trees
This tells you where you can see one of the biggest examples of the species in Britain.

Fact file
Provides vital statistics and information.

Leaf and twig
Use the leaf and twig to help identify the tree in summer or winter. (Evergreens do not have a winter twig because they don't lose their leaves.)

Black poplar *Populus nigra*

OVAL

Once common along riverbanks, today the native black poplar is very rare and found only in southern England and parts of Ireland. Black poplars are either male or female. Only a few hundred female trees exist in Britain and few of them grow near males. This means that seeds are rarely produced, so new trees are hard to find. Arrows found on the wreck of the *Mary Rose* were made of black poplar wood – they had survived 400 years beneath the sea.

DECIDUOUS

CHAMPION TREE
CHRIST'S COLLEGE, POWYS
GIRTH 685 cm

HEIGHT 20–25 m
WHERE Southern England, Ireland; often near water
FLOWERING March/April
FRUITING April/May
LEAF TINT/FALL October
OTHER NAMES Water poplar
USES Boat-building, floorboards

smooth and tan coloured

male catkins are red and up to 6 cm long

seed capsules contain brown, cottony seeds

green female catkins develop into seed capsules

fine tooth on edge

shape can range from diamond to triangular

insects ○   birds ○   mammals ○   fungi ○   other   23

Illustrations
These show what the leaves, fruits and flowers of each species look like.

Tick list
Tick to record what you've seen on and around the tree.

MY OBSERVATIONS

Season:
_____

Where is the tree?
_____

_____

Describe the tree:
_____

_____

What wildlife can you see?
_____

_____

How tall is your tree?

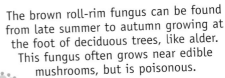

The brown roll-rim fungus can be found from late summer to autumn growing at the foot of deciduous trees, like alder. This fungus often grows near edible mushrooms, but is poisonous.

SEEN IT?

MEASURED IT?

MY DRAWINGS AND PHOTOS

On my tree I saw: leaves ○   buds ○   fruit ○   flowers ○

Alder *Alnus glutinosa*

The wood of the alder is fascinating — when it is submerged in water, it becomes as hard as stone. Much of the Italian city of Venice is built on piles of alder wood, which were sunk into the sand banks. Houses and other buildings were then built on top. The small, winged seeds of this water-loving tree get carried along by streams and rivers to grow further downstream. It is said that the green dye of the alder flower was used to colour the clothes of Robin Hood.

DECIDUOUS

HEIGHT 18–25 m

WHERE Widespread; woodland, hedgerows, often near water

FLOWERING February/March

FRUITING October–December

LEAF TINT/FALL November

OTHER NAMES Black alder, fearnog (Irish)

USES Canal lock gates, charcoal

smaller female catkins develop into cones

side buds are on short stalks

male catkins up to 5 cm long

toothed edges

mature cones are woody and open to release seeds

rounded leaf is shiny and dark

CHAMPION TREE
CHATSWORTH PARK,
DERBYSHIRE
GIRTH 609 cm

insects ○   birds ○   mammals ○   fungi ○   other . . . .

MY OBSERVATIONS

Season:

Where is the tree?

Describe the tree:

What wildlife can you see?

How tall is your tree?

SEEN IT?

MEASURED IT?

Great spotted woodpeckers are common in woodlands. Their colours and patterns make them easy to spot. Their tapping on tree trunks, including those of aspen, can be heard particularly in early spring.

MY DRAWINGS AND PHOTOS

On my tree I saw: leaves ○   buds ○   fruit ○   flowers ○

Aspen *Populus tremula*

Fluttering leaves, which tremble in the breeze, give the aspen its Latin name *tremula* and its common name of 'quaking aspen'. The autumn-dry leaves of the aspen produce a rustling noise even in gentle breezes. Herbalists once used its flowers to treat people suffering from anxiety or nightmares. In Medieval times, the timber was used to make houses for the poor who could not afford oak. Charcoal made from aspen wood was used in the production of gunpowder.

DECIDUOUS

HEIGHT 15–25 m

WHERE Widespread; hillsides, hedgerows, often near water

FLOWERING March

FRUITING May

LEAF TINT/FALL October

OTHER NAMES Quaking aspen

USES Matches, paper, boxes for fruit and vegetables

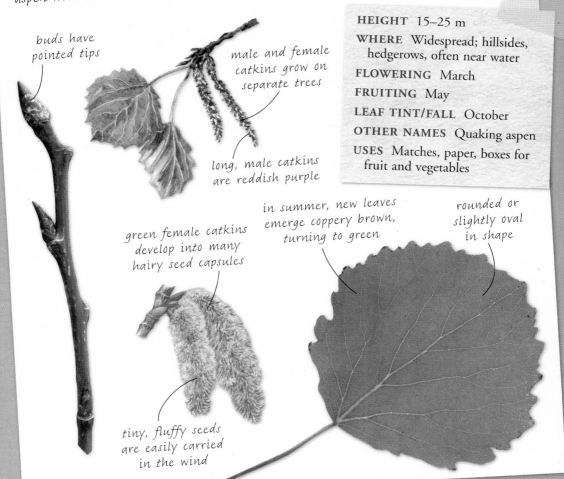

buds have pointed tips

male and female catkins grow on separate trees

long, male catkins are reddish purple

green female catkins develop into many hairy seed capsules

in summer, new leaves emerge coppery brown, turning to green

rounded or slightly oval in shape

tiny, fluffy seeds are easily carried in the wind

MY OBSERVATIONS

Season:

Where is the tree?

Describe the tree:

What wildlife can you see?

How tall is your tree?

Oyster fungi grow in forms called brackets on the trunks of beech and other deciduous trees. The topside is grey or cream, with white gills below. They are best seen in autumn.

SEEN IT?

MEASURED IT?

MY DRAWINGS AND PHOTOS

On my tree I saw: leaves ○   buds ○   fruit ○   flowers ○

Beech _Fagus sylvatica_

_B_eech trees have long been part of Britain's history, especially in the furniture-making industry. Particularly grand trees have been called 'queen beeches', and impressive beech woods are known as 'nature's cathedrals'. Since Roman times, beech wood was used for fuel and it was preferred for making furniture for its pink-orange colouring. Its nuts — called mast — were used as feed for animals.

DECIDUOUS

long, narrow buds

CHAMPION TREE
PLAS NEWYDD, ANGLESEY
GIRTH 962 cm

HEIGHT 10–35 m

WHERE Southern and eastern England, South Wales; woodland, chalky or sandy soils

FLOWERING April/May

FRUITING September–November

LEAF TINT/FALL November–April

OTHER NAMES Fea (Irish)

USES Furniture, kitchen utensils

female flowers are green and spiky on short stems

male flowers hang on long stems

glossy and dark green with a pointed tip

triangular, shiny, brown nuts are called mast

nuts are held in a prickly, four-lobed case

MY OBSERVATIONS

Season:
_____

Where is the tree?
_____

_____

Describe the tree:
_____

_____

What wildlife can you see?
_____

_____

How tall is your tree? _____

_____

MEASURED IT?

SEEN IT?

The striking hornet moth is rare in the UK. Adult moths lay their eggs in poplar trees, including black poplar. The larvae hatch and burrow into the wood, developing into adults in June and July.

MY DRAWINGS AND PHOTOS

On my tree I saw: leaves ○   buds ○   fruit ○   flowers ○

Black poplar *Populus nigra*

Once common along riverbanks, today the native black poplar is very rare and found only in southern England and parts of Ireland. Black poplars are either male or female. Only a few hundred female trees exist in Britain and few of them grow near males. This means that seeds are rarely produced, so new trees are hard to find. Arrows found on the wreck of the *Mary Rose* were made of black poplar wood — they had survived 400 years beneath the sea.

DECIDUOUS

CHAMPION TREE
CHRIST'S COLLEGE, POWYS
GIRTH 685 cm

HEIGHT 20–25 m
WHERE Southern England, Ireland; often near water
FLOWERING March/April
FRUITING April/May
LEAF TINT/FALL October
OTHER NAMES Water poplar
USES Boat-building, floorboards

smooth and tan coloured

shape can range from diamond to triangular

fine tooth on edge

male catkins are red and up to 6 cm long

green female catkins develop into seed capsules

seed capsules contain brown, cottony seeds

MY OBSERVATIONS

Season: _____

Where is the tree? _____

_____

Describe the tree: _____

_____

What wildlife can you see? _____

_____

How tall is your tree? _____

_____

SEEN IT?

MEASURED IT?

Dunnocks, also known as hedge sparrows, find shelter and berries to eat amongst blackthorn. Its branches grow tangled and spiny, making blackthorn a good tree for birds to build their nests.

MY DRAWINGS AND PHOTOS

On my tree I saw: leaves ○   buds ○   fruit ○   flowers ○

Blackthorn *Prunus spinosa*

This deciduous tree is distinctive because its flowers are some of the first to appear in spring, appearing even before its leaves. The fruits of the blackthorn are known as sloes and, although bitter to taste, they are popular with birds. It has long been considered a magical tree. In Celtic mythology it was home to fairies, and a blackthorn staff (long stick) was thought to be ideal for keeping evil spirits away.

DECIDUOUS

fruits, called sloes, are blue-black

sharply pointed, stiff spines

tiny flowers emerge before the leaves

white, scented flowers have five petals

leaf is dull green in colour and between 2 to 4 cm long

dark, almost black in colour, and spiny

finely toothed edge

HEIGHT 6–7 m

WHERE Widespread; woodland, scrubland, hedgerows

FLOWERING March/April

FRUITING August/September

LEAF TINT/FALL October/November

OTHER NAMES Sloe

USES Walking sticks, fruits used in food and drink

insects ○   birds ○   mammals ○   fungi ○   other . . . .

MY OBSERVATIONS

Season: _____

Where is the tree? _____

_____

Describe the tree: _____

_____

_____

What wildlife can you see? _____

_____

_____

How tall is your tree? _____

MEASURED IT?

SEEN IT?

Box suckers are insects that spend winter as eggs on a box plant, hatching in spring. The larvae suck the tree's sap, making chemicals that stop the plant growing. Adults develop May to June.

MY DRAWINGS AND PHOTOS

On my tree I saw: leaves ○   buds ○   fruit ○   flowers ○

Box *Buxus sempervirens*

Slow-growing and never gaining great height, box is considered to be more of a shrub than a tree. Its small, glossy, evergreen leaves grow tightly together, making it a perfect plant for garden hedges. Box can be cut and shaped into ornamental bushes in a practice known as topiary. It has an unpleasant smell, which caused Queen Anne (1665–1714) to have it removed from the gardens of Hampton Court Palace. Although common in gardens, box is rare in the wild.

EVERGREEN

HEIGHT 6–8 m

WHERE Southern England; gardens, chalky soils

FLOWERING January–May

FRUITING August/September

LEAF TINT/FALL Evergreen

OTHER NAMES Common box, boxwood

USES Kitchen tools, engraving

leaves are 1.5 to 3 cm long on hairy twigs

male and female flowers grow together in clusters

three-horned, woody seed capsules are up to 8 mm long

male flowers are yellow, female flowers are greenish

small, tough and glossy

seed capsules open to release several black seeds

MY OBSERVATIONS

Season: _____

Where is the tree? _____

_____

Describe the tree: _____

_____

_____

What wildlife can you see? _____

_____

_____

How tall is your tree? _____

_____

Brimstone butterflies lay their eggs on buckthorn leaves as this is the only plant eaten by the larvae. Adults hibernate over the winter and are one of the first butterflies to be seen in spring.

SEEN IT?

MEASURED IT?

MY DRAWINGS AND PHOTOS

On my tree I saw: leaves ○   buds ○   fruit ○   flowers ○

Buckthorn *Rhamnus cathartica*

n the past, plants and trees were used to treat illnesses and buckthorn is no exception. The ripe, black berries are mildly poisonous to humans, but they are a good source of food for many birds. When herbal remedies were common, a tea made from buckthorn berries was used to treat a stomach ache, even though it causes vomiting and diarrhoea! Because of this, it is also referred to as purging buckthorn. The bark of a young tree is orange-brown and darkens with age.

DECIDUOUS

HEIGHT 4–6 m

WHERE Widespread; hedgerows, woodland

FLOWERING May/June

FRUITING September/October

LEAF TINT/FALL October/ November

OTHER NAMES Common buckthorn, purging buckthorn

USES Carving, kitchen utensils

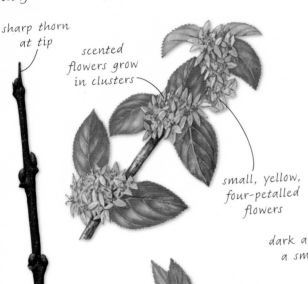

sharp thorn at tip

scented flowers grow in clusters

small, yellow, four-petalled flowers

dark and glossy with a smooth surface

each berry contains two to four seeds

shiny, black berries (fruits) are up to 8 mm long

MY OBSERVATIONS

Season:
_____

Where is the tree?
_____
_____

Describe the tree:
_____
_____
_____

What wildlife can you see?
_____
_____

How tall is your tree?
_____

SEEN IT?

MEASURED IT?

The yellow-green lime aphid, *eucallipterus tiliae*, can be seen during the spring and summer months. Aphids are often regarded as pests because they feed on the tree's sap and can spread viruses.

MY DRAWINGS AND PHOTOS

On my tree I saw: leaves ○   buds ○   fruit ○   flowers ○

Common lime *Tilia x europaea (vulgaris)*

The widely planted common lime is easy to spot as its leaves, and anything under them, get covered in a sticky substance called honeydew. Tiny insects called aphids suck sap (a sugary liquid) from the tree and produce honeydew. This attracts dirt, and by autumn, the leaves are sticky and filthy – and so are cars that may be parked beneath its branches. Beekeepers often place their hives near lime trees so that the bees produce 'lime honey'.

DECIDUOUS

CHAMPION TREE

HOLKER HALL, CUMBRIA
GIRTH 789 cm

red buds

HEIGHT 20–40 m

WHERE Widespread; woodland, parks, gardens, streets

FLOWERING July

FRUITING September

LEAF TINT/FALL October/November

OTHER NAMES Common linden

USES Carving, model-building, guitar making

small, yellow, five-petalled flowers

scented groups of flowers hang on long stalks

5 to 10 cm long with a pointed tip

slightly heart-shaped with tufts of hair on the underside

an extra leaflet, called a bract, helps the fruits to travel in the wind

small, hard, round fruits

insects ○   birds ○   mammals ○   fungi ○   other . . . .

MY OBSERVATIONS

Season: _____

Where is the tree? _____

_____

Describe the tree: _____

_____

_____

What wildlife can you see? _____

_____

_____

How tall is your tree? _____

_____

The autumn fruits of the crab apple tree attract greenfinches, along with many other birds. Greenfinches gather together in large flocks to feed, making lots of noise as they call to one another.

SEEN IT?

MEASURED IT?

MY DRAWINGS AND PHOTOS

On my tree I saw: leaves ○   buds ○   fruit ○   flowers ○

Crab apple *Malus sylvestis*

Crab apples have been cultivated (grown especially) for hundreds of years, but a truly wild tree can be told apart by its thorns. These trees produce small, sour apples that are not good to eat raw. However, they are often made into tasty crab apple jellies and jams. Crab apple wood is hard, heavy and strong, making it ideal for items that endure heavy wear, such as tools and handles. The wood produces a pleasant scent when burnt.

DECIDUOUS

HEIGHT 7–9 m

WHERE Widespread, except Scotland; woodland, hedgerows

FLOWERING April/May

FRUITING September/October

LEAF TINT/FALL October/ November

OTHER NAMES Wild crab

USES Carving, mallets, tool handles, fruits made into jelly

flowers are up to 4 cm across and grow in clusters

white petals are tinged pink

reddish-brown with small buds (wild trees also have thorns)

toothed edges and a pointed tip

young fruits are yellow-green, ripe fruits are rosy-red

apples grow up to 4 cm in diameter

long stalk

MY OBSERVATIONS

Season: _____

Where is the tree? _____

_____

Describe the tree: _____

_____

_____

What wildlife can you see? _____

_____

_____

How tall is your tree? _____

_____

Robins often build their nests in hedgerows, including those of dogwood. Two broods of up to six blue eggs are laid from April to August. The berries also provide food for robins in autumn.

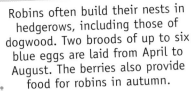

SEEN IT?

MEASURED IT?

MY DRAWINGS AND PHOTOS

On my tree I saw: leaves ○   buds ○   fruit ○   flowers ○

Dogwood *Cornus sanguinea*

This small tree or shrub has red-tinted stems that are especially noticeable in winter when there are few colours to brighten the dark days. Dogwood has nothing to do with dogs. The wood is hard and was once used to make skewers known as 'dags'. This gave the tree its old name of dagswood. The leaves of dogwood can be identified by gently pulling them apart – a stringy latex can be seen where the veins have been broken.

DECIDUOUS

reddish in colour

small, white flowers have four petals and are up to 1 cm across

bad-smelling flowers grow in clusters

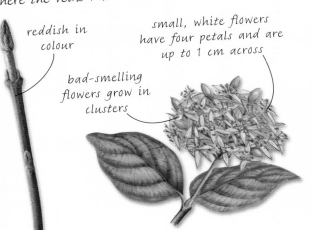

HEIGHT 2–5 m

WHERE Widespread; woodland, scrubland, hedgerows

FLOWERING May/June

FRUITING September–November

LEAF TINT/FALL October/November

OTHER NAMES Bloodtwig

USES Skewers, arrow shafts, lamp oil can be made from fruits

smooth edges and deep veins with a pointed tip

fruits are black, pea-sized berries

berries are bitter to taste and not good to eat

leaves turn dark red in autumn

MY OBSERVATIONS

Season: _____

Where is the tree? _____

_____

Describe the tree: _____

_____

_____

What wildlife can you see? _____

_____

_____

How tall is your tree? _____

_____

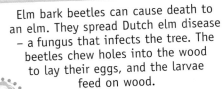

Elm bark beetles can cause death to an elm. They spread Dutch elm disease – a fungus that infects the tree. The beetles chew holes into the wood to lay their eggs, and the larvae feed on wood.

SEEN IT?

MEASURED IT?

MY DRAWINGS AND PHOTOS

On my tree I saw: leaves ○   buds ○   fruit ○   flowers ○

English elm *Ulmus procera*

English elms were common in Britain, until the onset of Dutch elm disease killed 25 million of them in the 1970s. It is thought that this tree was introduced to Britain 2000 years ago by the Romans, and some scientific research suggests that all English elms descended from just one tree. This meant that many elms were equally vulnerable in the face of disease. Today, elms can often be seen growing in hedgerows.

DECIDUOUS

thick and reddish in colour

purple flowers are in small clusters

flowers appear before the leaves

HEIGHT 16–30 m

WHERE Widespread; woodland, hedgerows

FLOWERING February/March

FRUITING April–June

LEAF TINT/FALL October/November

OTHER NAMES Field elm

USES Before metal, the wood was used for water pipes

papery, winged fruits contain one seed each

one side is longer than the other

fruits are on short stalks

toothed edges

insects ○ birds ○ mammals ○ fungi ○ other . . . .

MY OBSERVATIONS

Season: _____

Where is the tree? _____

_____

Describe the tree: _____

_____

_____

What wildlife can you see? _____

_____

_____

How tall is your tree? _____

_____

SEEN IT?

MEASURED IT?

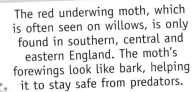

The red underwing moth, which is often seen on willows, is only found in southern, central and eastern England. The moth's forewings look like bark, helping it to stay safe from predators.

MY DRAWINGS AND PHOTOS

On my tree I saw: leaves ○   buds ○   fruit ○   flowers ○

Goat willow *Salix caprea*

The goat willow is also known as 'pussy willow' because its springtime male catkins are soft and grey – like a cat's paw. Goat willows are important trees in woodland and hedgerows because they are closely associated with many types of butterfly and moth. Some larvae feed on the leaves and others live under the bark, feeding on the wood. As male catkins mature and turn yellow they are called 'goslings' because they are the same colour as baby geese.

DECIDUOUS

HEIGHT 4–10 m

WHERE Widespread; woodland, hedgerows

FLOWERING March/April

FRUITING May

LEAF TINT/FALL October/November

OTHER NAMES Pussy willow, great swallow

USES Stems are used in basket-making

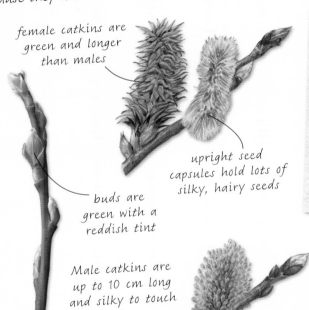

female catkins are green and longer than males

upright seed capsules hold lots of silky, hairy seeds

buds are green with a reddish tint

Male catkins are up to 10 cm long and silky to touch

long and oval

grey at first, turning to yellow

male and female catkins appear on different trees

dull green, and slightly hairy on upper surface

insects ○ birds ○ mammals ○ fungi ○ other . . . .

MY OBSERVATIONS

Season: _____

Where is the tree? _____

_____

Describe the tree: _____

_____

_____

What wildlife can you see? _____

_____

_____

How tall is your tree? _____

_____

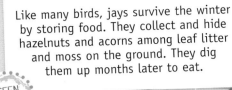

Like many birds, jays survive the winter by storing food. They collect and hide hazelnuts and acorns among leaf litter and moss on the ground. They dig them up months later to eat.

SEEN IT?

MEASURED IT?

MY DRAWINGS AND PHOTOS

On my tree I saw: leaves ○   buds ○   fruit ○   flowers ○

Hazel *Corylus avellana*

$\Large A$s hazel catkins turn yellow it's a sign that spring is coming, and when squirrels start to gather hazelnuts winter is just around the corner. Hazels are not only a source of food for many types of wildlife, they provide homes and shelter for them too. They often grow in dense clusters with lots of stems growing from the ground, rather than a single trunk.

DECIDUOUS

CHAMPION TREE
STOURHEAD, WILTSHIRE
GIRTH 248 cm

HEIGHT 12–15 m

WHERE Widespread; woodland, scrubland, hedgerows

FLOWERING February

FRUITING August/September

LEAF TINT/FALL November

OTHER NAMES Coll (Irish)

USES Walking sticks, stems used for fences and baskets

stiff hairs and small, oval buds

female flowers look like buds with tiny, red tassels

long, drooping male catkins are known as 'lambs' tails'

toothed edges and slightly hairy

fruits are smooth, round, woody nuts

nuts sit in a ragged, green or brown, leafy husk

short stalk

insects ○   birds ○   mammals ○   fungi ○   other . . . .

MY OBSERVATIONS

Season: _____

Where is the tree? _____

_____

Describe the tree: _____

_____

_____

What wildlife can you see? _____

_____

_____

How tall is your tree? _____

_____

SEEN IT?

MEASURED IT?

Hawfinches can often be seen perching in the tops of trees, such as hornbeam. These birds have large, powerful bills that they use to crack open the hornbeam's tough nuts.

MY DRAWINGS AND PHOTOS

On my tree I saw: leaves ○   buds ○   fruit ○   flowers ○

Hornbeam *Carpinus betulus*

The statuesque hornbeam is an impressive deciduous tree with its pale, silvery-grey bark, and yellow-green catkins in the spring. It's often coppiced (stems cut back to the ground causing many long shoots to grow) or pollarded (top branches cut) and it is commonly planted for hedging. The white wood is very fine-grained, which makes particularly good firewood and charcoal. The Romans made their chariots from this wood because of its strength.

DECIDUOUS

CHAMPION TREE

HATFIELD FOREST, ESSEX
GIRTH 450 cm

long buds

male catkins are yellow-green with red specks

HEIGHT 10–20 m

WHERE Southern and eastern England; woodland, hedgerows

FLOWERING March

FRUITING September

LEAF TINT/FALL November–April

OTHER NAMES Musclewood, ironwood

USES Chopping blocks, charcoal

green female catkins develop into fruits

fruits are tough nuts with a three-lobed leaflet, or bract, attached

double-toothed edge with pointed tip

MY OBSERVATIONS

Season: _____

Where is the tree? _____

_____

Describe the tree: _____

_____

_____

What wildlife can you see? _____

_____

_____

How tall is your tree? _____

_____

MEASURED IT?

SEEN IT?

The seven-spotted ladybird is the most common ladybird in Europe. From February, they can be seen on plants, and trees such as mulberrys. Ladybirds hibernate in groups during winter.

MY DRAWINGS AND PHOTOS

On my tree I saw: leaves ○   buds ○   fruit ○   flowers ○

Mulberry *Morus nigra*

The black mulberry tree has a long history rooted in Southeast Asia, where it has been cultivated for thousands of years. It was introduced to Europe by the Romans, who dedicated the tree to Minerva, their goddess of wisdom. It has been widely planted and is grown in sheltered gardens for its delicious fruits, which contain a staining dye. It is celebrated in the nursery rhyme, 'Here we go round the mulberry bush'.

DECIDUOUS

HEIGHT 8–10 m

WHERE England; mostly gardens

FLOWERING May

FRUITING July

LEAF TINT/FALL October/November

OTHER NAMES Black mulberry, Persian mulberry, sycamine tree

USES Fruits are eaten raw or made into jam

buds are broad and pointed

green female flowers are 1 to 2 cm long

male flowers are yellow-green and longer than the female flowers

rough to touch on upper side

raspberry-like fruits are purple-red and sweet when ripe

toothed edges

insects ○ birds ○ mammals ○ fungi ○ other . . . .

45

MY OBSERVATIONS

Season: _____

Where is the tree? _____

_____

Describe the tree: _____

_____

_____

What wildlife can you see? _____

_____

_____

How tall is your tree? _____

_____

SEEN IT?

MEASURED IT?

Comma butterflies fly in late summer and early autumn and sometimes feed on fallen fruits, such as apples, pears and plums. The caterpillars feed on nettle, elm and hazel shoots.

MY DRAWINGS AND PHOTOS

On my tree I saw: leaves ⭕   buds ⭕   fruit ⭕   flowers ⭕

Pear *Pyrus communis*

DECIDUOUS

The pear tree originally came from Southwest Asia, but it is now common throughout Europe. Pears have undergone many changes since they first arrived in Europe as farmers have cultivated sweeter and juicier varieties of the fruit. Pear trees can be found in gardens and orchards in Britain, especially southern areas. The wild pear, which is a different type of pear, is rare, and its fruits are hard, gritty and smaller than those of the *Pyrus communis*.

HEIGHT 9–15 m

WHERE Southern England; orchards, woodland, gardens

FLOWERING March/April

FRUITING September/October

LEAF TINT/FALL November

OTHER NAMES Common pear, European pear

USES Wood is turned on a lathe to make bowls and similar objects

hard fruits (pears) up to 12 cm long

ripe pears are yellow-green, sometimes rosy

reddish-brown and hairy when young

up to 8 cm in length with a pointed tip

flowers have five pure-white petals

centres are pink-purple

smooth or finely toothed edge

MY OBSERVATIONS

Season: _____

Where is the tree? _____

_____

Describe the tree: _____

_____

_____

What wildlife can you see? _____

_____

_____

How tall is your tree? _____

_____

MEASURED IT?

The larvae of the November moth feed on a wide range of trees, including plum and birch. Adult moths are hard to spot because their mottled grey-brown wings are perfectly camouflaged against bark.

SEEN IT?

MY DRAWINGS AND PHOTOS

On my tree I saw: leaves ○   buds ○   fruit ○   flowers ○

Plum *Prunus domestica*

Plum trees are most commonly found growing in orchards and gardens. Plums were probably created as a hybrid (mix) of blackthorn and cherry plum. Today, plums are the second-most cultivated fruit in the world. The plum *Prunus domestica* is first mentioned in 479 BC in the writings of the Chinese philosopher Confucius — it is listed as a popular food in Chinese culture. A tree will not produce fruit until it is four or five years old. Dried fruits are known as prunes.

DECIDUOUS

HEIGHT 8–10 m

LIFESPAN 20–40 years

WHERE Mainly England; orchards, gardens

FLOWERING April/May

FRUITING July–September

LEAF TINT/FALL October/ November

OTHER NAMES European plum

USES Grown for fruit

smooth skin

purple fruits are large, round and juicy

clusters of flowers

flowers are white, sometimes tinged with green

finely toothed edges

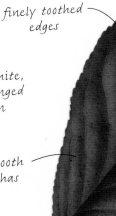

upper surface is smooth and lower surface has tiny hairs

smooth and brown

insects ○   birds ○   mammals ○   fungi ○   other . . . .

MY OBSERVATIONS

Season: _____

Where is the tree? _____

_____

Describe the tree: _____

_____

_____

What wildlife can you see? _____

_____

_____

How tall is your tree? _____

_____

MEASURED IT?

SEEN IT?

The birch polypore fungus grows on the trunks of birch trees in a shape called a bracket. Unlike plants that use photosynthesis, fungi take nourishment from the tree using tiny organs called 'hyphae'.

MY DRAWINGS AND PHOTOS

On my tree I saw: leaves ○   buds ○   fruit ○   flowers ○

Silver birch *Betula pendula*

With its silvery bark and fluttering leaves, the silver birch is sometimes called 'Queen of the forest'. It was one of the first trees to start growing back in Britain at the end of the Ice Age, around 10,000 years ago. It is known as a pioneer species, which means it is one of the first plants to grow in a new area. Silver birch produces huge crops of seeds of up to one million every year. This tree is easily recognisable by its bark, even in the winter.

DECIDUOUS

CHAMPION TREE
PRIORY PARK, SURREY
GIRTH 399 cm

HEIGHT 18–25 m

WHERE Widespread; woodland, scrubland

FLOWERING April/May

FRUITING June

LEAF TINT/FALL November

OTHER NAMES Warty birch, beith (Irish)

USES Cotton reels

slender green female catkins develop into seed capsules

brown with small bumps, or warts

double-toothed edges

winged seeds, 1 to 2 mm long, are released from the fruits

male catkins are long, drooping and yellow

stalks are 1 to 2 cm long

MY OBSERVATIONS

Season: _____

Where is the tree? _____

_____

Describe the tree: _____

_____

_____

What wildlife can you see? _____

_____

_____

How tall is your tree? _____

_____

The green hairstreak butterfly can often be seen on plants, such as the wayfaring tree, searching for flowers. Like many butterflies, the adults feed on nectar – a sweet liquid produced by flowers.

SEEN IT?

MEASURED IT?

MY DRAWINGS AND PHOTOS

On my tree I saw: leaves ○   buds ○   fruit ○   flowers ○

Wayfaring tree *Viburnum lantana*

Once common alongside footpaths in southern England, the wayfaring tree grows in hedgerows, scrubland or on chalky ground. Today, it is a more common sight in gardens, grown for its ornamental leaves, large flower heads and bright berries. Despite their attractive appearance, the berries are mildly poisonous and should not be eaten. The young, flexible stems can be used to make twine.

DECIDUOUS

grey-brown and hairy

fruits are oval berries that turn black when ripe

berries are up to 8 mm long

HEIGHT Up to 6 m

WHERE South England, south Wales; hedgerows, scrubland, chalky soils

FLOWERING May

FRUITING August/September

LEAF TINT/FALL October/ November

OTHER NAMES Hoarwithy

USES Young shoots can be made into twine

rough upper surface with deep veins

flowers have five petals

white flowers appear in dense clusters

underside is hairy

MY OBSERVATIONS

Season: _____

Where is the tree? _____

_____

Describe the tree: _____

_____

_____

What wildlife can you see? _____

_____

_____

How tall is your tree? _____

_____

SEEN IT?

MEASURED IT?

Whitebeam berries attract many birds, including waxwings, which are winter visitors to Britain. These unusually tame birds have crests on their heads and waxy red spots on their wings.

MY DRAWINGS AND PHOTOS

On my tree I saw: leaves ○   buds ○   fruit ○   flowers ○

Whitebeam _Sorbus aria_

DECIDUOUS

When the leaves of the whitebeam first open in the spring they appear white, giving this tree its name ('beam' is the Saxon word for tree). The whiteness is caused by the young leaves' soft coating of white hairs. Hair on the topside soon disappears as the leaves mature and droop downwards, but the undersides stay white. The wood of the whitebeam is very hard-wearing, and its small, red fruits can be made into jam and wine.

HEIGHT 8–15 m

WHERE Southern England; woodland, chalky soils

FLOWERING May/June

FRUITING September

LEAF TINT/FALL October/ November

OTHER NAMES Common whitebeam

USES Tool handles, furniture

green buds

loose clusters of white flowers

each berry contains two seeds

fruits are oval-shaped berries that turn red when ripe

leaf is up to 8 cm long

white hairs on underside

MY OBSERVATIONS

Season: _____

Where is the tree? _____

_____

Describe the tree: _____

_____

_____

What wildlife can you see? _____

_____

_____

How tall is your tree? _____

_____

MEASURED IT?

SEEN IT?

Blackbirds are just one of many birds that flock around fruiting cherry trees to feed on their sweet fruits. Males are black with yellow beaks, and females are brown with spotted undersides.

MY DRAWINGS AND PHOTOS

On my tree I saw: leaves ○   buds ○   fruit ○   flowers ○

Wild cherry *Prunus avium*

When its branches are laden with white flowers or bunches of glossy fruits, the wild cherry attracts many birds. According to folklore, this tree has particular associations with cuckoos. The birds are believed to need three good meals of cherries before they will stop singing. The wood of a cherry tree is fine-grained and a beautiful shade of red, making it popular with cabinet makers.

DECIDUOUS

CHAMPION TREE
STUDLEY ROYAL & FOUNTAINS ABBEY, YORKSHIRE
GIRTH 572 cm

HEIGHT 18–25 m

WHERE Widespread; parks, woodland

FLOWERING April/May

FRUITING July/August

LEAF TINT/FALL October/November

OTHER NAMES Gean, crann silin (Irish)

USES Furniture, veneers (thin layer of wood used in furniture-making)

brown-red buds

white, five-petalled flowers grow in groups of up to six

toothed edges

berry-like fruits ripen to red

up to 15 cm in length, with a long, pointed tip

MY OBSERVATIONS

Season: _____

Where is the tree? _____

_____

Describe the tree: _____

_____

_____

What wildlife can you see? _____

_____

_____

How tall is your tree? _____

_____

SEEN IT?

MEASURED IT?

The privet hawk moth lays its eggs on the leaves of privet, ash and lilac. When the larvae hatch, they feed on the leaves. Its wings and body have pink, white and brown markings.

MY DRAWINGS AND PHOTOS

On my tree I saw: leaves ○   buds ○   fruit ○   flowers ○

Wild privet *Ligustrum vulgare*

For centuries, gardeners have taken wild trees and shrubs, such as privet, and grown them as ornamental plants. Privet is one of few trees and shrubs that is described as being semi-evergreen. Depending on climate, sometimes it loses its leaves in winter and sometimes it doesn't. Privet is commonly grown in gardens and cut neatly into hedges, but the wild form looks very different, with long branches that reach upwards. The flowers and fruits were once used to treat eye and mouth diseases, despite being poisonous.

SEMI-EVERGREEN

HEIGHT 3–5 m

WHERE Southern and central England, Wales; gardens, streets, parks

FLOWERING May/June

FRUITING September/October

LEAF TINT/FALL Semi-evergreen

USES Planted for hedges

flowers grow in cone-shaped clusters

flowers develop into fruits

cream-coloured, sweet-scented flowers attract insects

fruits are shiny, black berries

young twigs are covered in short hairs

MY OBSERVATIONS

Season: _____

Where is the tree? _____

_____

Describe the tree: _____

_____

_____

What wildlife can you see? _____

_____

_____

How tall is your tree? _____

MEASURED IT?

_____

SEEN IT?

White-letter hairstreak butterflies only breed on elm. When these trees were struck down by disease in the 1970s, butterfly numbers dropped dramatically. The larvae of this butterfly are green.

MY DRAWINGS AND PHOTOS

On my tree I saw: leaves ○   buds ○   fruit ○   flowers ○

Wych elm *Ulmus glabra*

In Middle English (a language spoken long ago) the word 'wych' meant bendy. Wych elm trees are not particularly bendy, but their young shoots are and they can be bent and twisted for making into baskets and other goods. These trees were badly affected by Dutch elm disease – a fungus carried by a wood-boring beetle. The leaves of the Wych elm are the largest of any native tree and can be up to 18 cm long!

DECIDUOUS

flat, winged fruits are 2 cm long and contain one seed each

purplish flowers grow in clusters

twelve to eighteen pairs of veins, more than the English elm

covered in stiff hairs when young

uneven base, similar to the English elm

HEIGHT 16–30 m

WHERE Widespread; hedgerows, woodland

FLOWERING February/March

FRUITING May/June

LEAF TINT/FALL October/November

OTHER NAMES Scots elm

USES Chests, water troughs, sea defences

insects ○ birds ○ mammals ○ fungi ○ other . . . .

MY OBSERVATIONS

Season:

Where is the tree?

Describe the tree:

What wildlife can you see?

How tall is your tree?

Holly blue butterflies lay two broods in the summer. The first brood is laid on holly and the second is laid on ivy. Both the caterpillars (larvae) and the adults feed on the leaves of both plants.

SEEN IT?

MEASURED IT?

MY DRAWINGS AND PHOTOS

On my tree I saw: leaves ○   buds ○   fruit ○   flowers ○

Holly *Ilix aquifolium*

With its clusters of bright red berries and prickly leaves, the holly tree is steeped in myth and mystery and is the subject of many superstitions. Although it was thought that cutting holly would bring bad luck, the custom of bringing holly into the home at midwinter goes back thousands of years. Hanging holly was thought to ward off evil spirits, and with its evergreen leaves, this tree was thought to symbolise fertility and be an effective charm against witches and goblins.

EVERGREEN

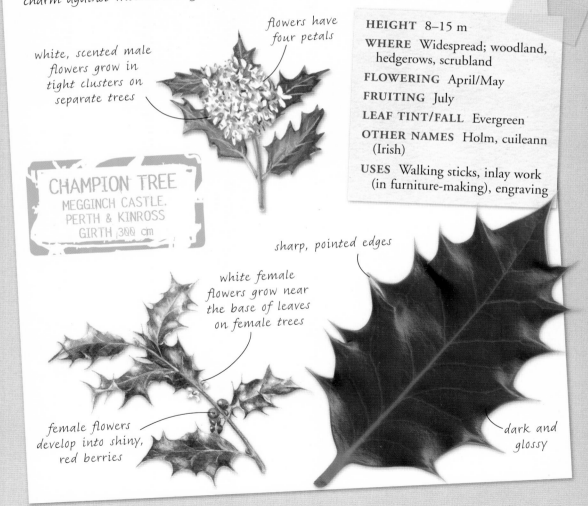

flowers have four petals

white, scented male flowers grow in tight clusters on separate trees

HEIGHT 8–15 m

WHERE Widespread; woodland, hedgerows, scrubland

FLOWERING April/May

FRUITING July

LEAF TINT/FALL Evergreen

OTHER NAMES Holm, cuileann (Irish)

USES Walking sticks, inlay work (in furniture-making), engraving

CHAMPION TREE
MEGGINCH CASTLE,
PERTH & KINROSS
GIRTH 300 cm

sharp, pointed edges

white female flowers grow near the base of leaves on female trees

female flowers develop into shiny, red berries

dark and glossy

insects ○   birds ○   mammals ○   fungi ○   other . . . .

MY OBSERVATIONS

Season: _____

Where is the tree? _____

_____

Describe the tree: _____

_____

What wildlife can you see? _____

_____

How tall is your tree? _____

_____

SEEN IT?

MEASURED IT?

Wild rabbits are grey-brown in colour and are very common in the British countryside. In winter, when there is less food, they sometimes gnaw the bark of trees, including magnolia.

MY DRAWINGS AND PHOTOS

On my tree I saw:　　leaves ○　　buds ○　　fruit ○　　flowers ○

Magnolia *Magnolia grandiflora*

With their enormous, fragrant blooms and clusters of red seeds, magnolias are impressive trees that brighten up a garden. They originally came from the United States and are the state flowers of Mississippi and Louisiana. Magnolias are normally fertilised by beetles. Its petals are unusually tough, which minimises damage by the crawling insects. They are named after Pierre Magnol (1638–1715), a French botanist, and many different varieties have been cultivated.

EVERGREEN

HEIGHT 12–25 m

WHERE Widespread; gardens, parks, arboretums

FLOWERING June–August

FRUITING September–December

LEAF TINT/FALL Evergreen

OTHER NAMES Southern evergreen magnolia

USES Veneers, vegetable crates

six to twelve petals

large, white, scented flowers up to 25 cm across

furry seed capsules are up to 6 cm long and turn from green to pink

seed capsules open to release red seeds

thick and glossy with smooth edges

up to 16 cm long

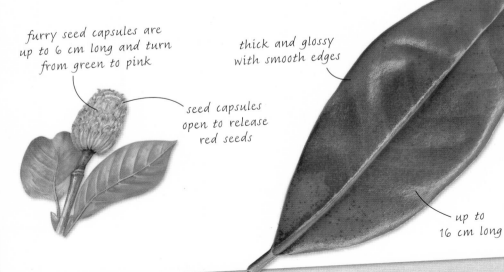

insects ○ birds ○ mammals ○ fungi ○ other . . . .

65

MY OBSERVATIONS

Season: _____

Where is the tree? _____

_____

Describe the tree: _____

_____

_____

What wildlife can you see? _____

_____

_____

How tall is your tree? _____

_____

MEASURED IT?

The gall wasp lays its eggs inside the oak tree. As a larva grows, a protective growth forms around it called a gall, or 'oak apple'. The larva stays inside the gall until it has developed into an adult.

SEEN IT?

MY DRAWINGS AND PHOTOS

On my tree I saw: leaves ○   buds ○   fruit ○   flowers ○

Pedunculate oak *Quercus robur*

The pedunculate, or English, oak is known as the 'king of the forest' and it has a rich history, featuring in many myths and legends. English oaks provide a unique habitat for hundreds of species of other plants and animals. Oaks attract insects, which in turn attract birds, and acorns provide food for squirrels and other small mammals. A single tree can live for hundreds of years.

DECIDUOUS

up to
3 cm long

HEIGHT 15–25 m

WHERE Widespread; ancient woodland

FLOWERING May

FRUITING October

LEAF TINT/FALL November

OTHER NAMES Common oak, dair (Irish), English oak

USES Building, furniture, floorboards

cluster of
buds at
the tip

acorns (fruits) sit in cups at
the end of long stalks, unlike
the acorns of the sessile oak,
which don't have stalks

three to six
rounded lobes
on each side

male catkins
are green-yellow

CHAMPION TREE
BOWTHORPE PARK FARM,
LINCOLNSHIRE
GIRTH 1279 cm

almost
no stalk

insects ○   birds ○   mammals ○   fungi ○   other . . . .

MY OBSERVATIONS

Season:
_____

Where is the tree?
_____

_____

Describe the tree:
_____

_____

_____

What wildlife can you see?
_____

_____

How tall is your tree?
_____

_____

Fieldfares visit Britain in winter searching for food, and the berries from sea buckthorn are a good source. White flashes under their wings help identify these birds, which are a type of thrush.

SEEN IT?

MEASURED IT?

MY DRAWINGS AND PHOTOS

On my tree I saw: leaves ○   buds ○   fruit ○   flowers ○

Sea buckthorn *Hippophae rhamnoides*

This small, deciduous shrub can be found growing on exposed, windy coastlines in salty conditions that few other trees can tolerate. Sea buckthorn is an increasingly popular plant that is specially grown for the extraordinary properties of its bright orange berries and its deep and widespread roots. The berries are full of vitamin C and are used in skincare products. Its roots help to bind loose soil and add nitrogen to it, which is important for soil fertility.

DECIDUOUS

male flowers are up to 4 mm across and grow on separate trees to females

thorny, and develops silvery scales

green male flowers have leaf-like petals

HEIGHT 1–3 m

WHERE Widespread; coastal areas, sand dunes

FLOWERING March/April

FRUITING September

LEAF TINT/FALL November

USES Skewers, fruits used in herbal medicines and cosmetics

up to 6 cm long and 1 cm wide

fruits are bright orange berries that grow on the female trees

up to 8 mm long

silvery-green, long and slender

insects ○ birds ○ mammals ○ fungi ○ other . . . .

MY OBSERVATIONS

Season:

Where is the tree?

Describe the tree:

What wildlife can you see?

How tall is your tree?

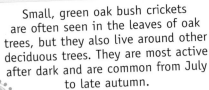

Small, green oak bush crickets are often seen in the leaves of oak trees, but they also live around other deciduous trees. They are most active after dark and are common from July to late autumn.

MY DRAWINGS AND PHOTOS

Sketch: Gardening Mag

On my tree I saw: leaves ○   buds ○   fruit ○   flowers ○

Sessile oak *Quercus petraea*

The sessile oak is one of just two native British oaks, but there are hundreds of different types in the northern hemisphere alone. The sessile oak is more likely to be found in stony uplands than the pedunculate oak, but they are similar in appearance. In Anglo-Saxon times, an oak was called an 'aik' and a seed was an 'aik-com', hence today's name – acorn. In one year, a mature oak tree may produce as many as 50,000 acorns.

DECIDUOUS

orange-brown buds

hard-shelled acorns (fruit) grow in clusters

sessile acorns do not have stalks, unlike pedunculate acorns, which have long stalks

HEIGHT 15–30 m

WHERE Widespread; hillsides, woodland

FLOWERING April/May

FRUITING October/November

LEAF TINT/FALL November/December

OTHER NAMES Durmast oak, dair (Irish) darachor (Gaelic)

USES Building, poles, fences

leaf stalks are 1 to 2 cm – much longer than those of the pedunculate oak

male catkins are yellow and drooping

CHAMPION TREE
COWDRAY PARK,
WEST SUSSEX
GIRTH 1253 cm

paler underneath with hairs on veins

insects ○   birds ○   mammals ○   fungi ○   other . . . .

MY OBSERVATIONS

Season: _____

Where is the tree? _____

_____

Describe the tree: _____

_____

_____

What wildlife can you see? _____

_____

_____

How tall is your tree? _____

_____

SEEN IT?

MEASURED IT?

Also known as the hawthorn fly, the St Mark's fly lives around meadows and hedgerows on shrubs, including spindle. The female adults begin hatching around April 25th, which is St Mark's Day.

MY DRAWINGS AND PHOTOS

On my tree I saw: leaves ○   buds ○   fruit ○   flowers ○

Spindle *Euonymus europaeus*

Spindles more often resemble bushes than trees, and they are often seen in hedgerows and woodlands. The timber of this plant was once used to make spindles – round, spinning pieces of wood that wool is wound onto. This gave the spindle tree its common name. The poisonous berries contain orange seeds that can be boiled to make a yellow dye. The berries have also been used in traditional remedies to cure farm animals of skin complaints.

DECIDUOUS

HEIGHT Up to 5 m

WHERE England, Wales; hedgerows, woodland

FLOWERING May/June

FRUITING September/October

LEAF TINT/FALL October/ November

OTHER NAMES Fusanum, fusoria, prickwood, skewerwood

USES Skewers, spindles, knitting needles

flowers have four green-white petals

green with shoots coming off at many angles

flowers grow in loose clusters

each seed pod is divided into four parts

long and oval-shaped with finely toothed edges

scarlet seed pods open to release four small, orange seeds

leaves turn orange and red in autumn

MY OBSERVATIONS

Season: _____

Where is the tree? _____

_____

Describe the tree: _____

_____

_____

What wildlife can you see? _____

_____

_____

How tall is your tree? _____

_____

SEEN IT?

MEASURED IT?

Grey squirrels have been commonly found in the UK, ever since they were introduced in the early 1900s. Their fur is grey, sometimes with brown tinges. Nutritious sweet chestnuts are one source of food for grey squirrels.

MY DRAWINGS AND PHOTOS

On my tree I saw: leaves ○   buds ○   fruit ○   flowers ○

Sweet chestnut *Castanea sativa*

These trees produce large, edible nuts that can be roasted and are often sold in streets, at fairs and other winter events. Sweet chestnuts have been long associated with winter festivals and were once seen as sources of magic. They are native to the warmer parts of Europe and were first brought to Britain by Roman soldiers, who relied on the nuts as an important part of their diet. Sweet chestnuts do not always ripen fully in Britain.

DECIDUOUS

CHAMPION TREE
CANFORD SCHOOL, DORSET
GIRTH 1,344 cm

long, male catkins can grow as long as the leaves

green, spiky female flowers grow at the base of the catkin

HEIGHT 20–30 m

WHERE Widespread; woodland, parks, well-drained soil

FLOWERING June/July

FRUITING October/November

LEAF TINT/FALL October–December

OTHER NAMES Spanish chestnut

USES Stems used for fence poles, nuts roasted for eating

sharply toothed edges

fruits open to reveal one to three glossy, brown nuts

tiny white dots, or warts, along twig

spiky, green casing

10 to 25 cm long

insects ○ birds ○ mammals ○ fungi ○ other . . . .

MY OBSERVATIONS

Season: _____

Where is the tree? _____

_____

Describe the tree: _____

_____

_____

What wildlife can you see? _____

_____

_____

How tall is your tree? _____

_____

SEEN IT?

MEASURED IT?

The beautiful song of a willow warbler marks the beginning of spring. These pretty birds visit Britain from April to October, and often perch in willow and birch trees looking for insects.

MY DRAWINGS AND PHOTOS

On my tree I saw: leaves ○   buds ○   fruit ○   flowers ○

White willow *Salix alba*

The white willow grows well in damp soil and so is most likely to be found alongside streams and ponds, often near alder trees. Animals, especially horses, enjoy nibbling the leaves and tender shoots of this tree. The pale brown wood of the white willow burns easily and quickly. This tree can be pollarded every four or five years to produce a crop of straight poles, which are used for making fences.

DECIDUOUS

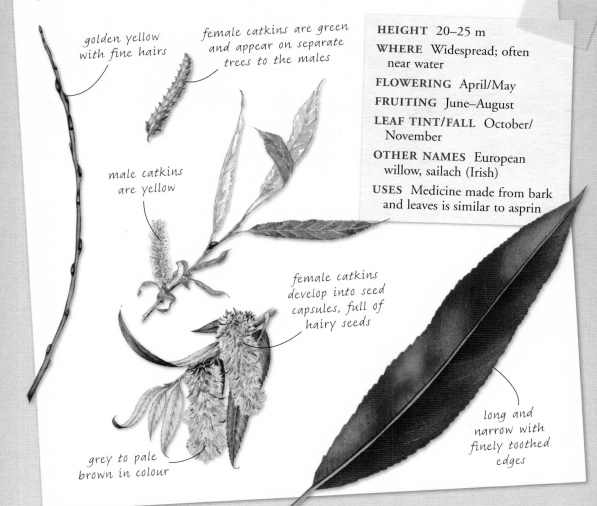

golden yellow with fine hairs

female catkins are green and appear on separate trees to the males

male catkins are yellow

female catkins develop into seed capsules, full of hairy seeds

grey to pale brown in colour

long and narrow with finely toothed edges

HEIGHT 20–25 m

WHERE Widespread; often near water

FLOWERING April/May

FRUITING June–August

LEAF TINT/FALL October/November

OTHER NAMES European willow, sailach (Irish)

USES Medicine made from bark and leaves is similar to asprin

insects ○   birds ○   mammals ○   fungi ○   other . . . .

MY OBSERVATIONS

Season: _____

Where is the tree? _____

_____

Describe the tree: _____

_____

_____

What wildlife can you see? _____

_____

_____

How tall is your tree? _____

_____

SEEN IT?

MEASURED IT?

Sycamore moths have a wingspan of up to 4.5 cm. They are pale to dark grey in colour, and have a mottled pattern that helps to camouflage them. These moths feed on sycamores, maples and horse chestnuts.

MY DRAWINGS AND PHOTOS

On my tree I saw: leaves ○   buds ○   fruit ○   flowers ○

Field Maple *Acer campestre*

The field maple provides an ideal habitat for many small creatures, and plants such as lichens and mosses. Field maples are often found growing in hedgerows. In autumn, they can be identified by their leaves, which turn red and yellow. According to ancient myths, a child could be guaranteed a long life by being passed through the branches of a field maple. In some places, it was thought that field maples could protect a house against bats.

DECIDUOUS

CHAMPION TREE
DOWNHAM CHURCHYARD,
ESSEX
GIRTH 452 cm

brown and coated in soft hairs

white-green flowers have five petals

HEIGHT 8–14 m

WHERE Widespread; woodland, hedgerows

FLOWERING April

FRUITING June/July

LEAF TINT/FALL November

OTHER NAMES Hedge maple, English maple

USES Wood used in violin-making

4 to 7 cm long, smaller than a sycamore

three to five rounded lobes

the wings are in a straight line, not curved as in the sycamore

paired, winged fruits are like helicopter blades

MY OBSERVATIONS

Season: _____

Where is the tree? _____

_____

Describe the tree: _____

_____

_____

What wildlife can you see? _____

_____

_____

How tall is your tree? _____

_____

SEEN IT?

MEASURED IT?

Bullfinches are shy birds that hide in thickets and hedges, such as guelder rose, but their low, clear whistle may give them away. They eat buds, berries and seeds.

MY DRAWINGS AND PHOTOS

On my tree I saw: leaves ○   buds ○   fruit ○   flowers ○

Guelder rose *Viburnum opulus*

Despite its name, this shrub is not a rose at all, but more closely related to the elder. Its unusual name comes from the Dutch province of Guelderland where it was grown as a decorative garden plant. Guelder rose berries are popular with birds, such as bullfinches, and small animals, but they are poisonous to humans. The berries can be used to make a red ink.

DECIDUOUS

buds grow in opposite pairs

central flowers develop into red berries

poisonous berries contain one seed each

HEIGHT Up to 4 m

WHERE Widespread; woodland, scrubland, hedgerows, damp soils

FLOWERING June/July

FRUITING September

LEAF TINT/FALL October/November

OTHER NAMES Snowball bush

USES Skewers

8 cm long with three large lobes

clusters of small, white flowers are encircled by larger white flowers

scented flowers have five petals

leaves turn reddish-brown in autumn

MY OBSERVATIONS

Season: _____

Where is the tree? _____

_____

Describe the tree: _____

_____

_____

What wildlife can you see? _____

_____

_____

How tall is your tree? _____

_____

SEEN IT?

MEASURED IT?

The hawthorn shield bug has brown markings on its broad, shield-shaped back. It's common on hawthorn leaves, but also feeds on other types of shrub and tree, including oaks and whitebeam.

MY DRAWINGS AND PHOTOS

On my tree I saw: leaves ○   buds ○   fruit ○   flowers ○

Hawthorn *Crataegus monogyna*

The hawthorn's frothy white blossom is a sign that summer is on its way. Hawthorn is a popular hedgerow plant and its leaves are quick to appear in spring. In folklore, in North Wales, hawthorn was associated with death, possibly because the flowers' scent reminds some people of rotting flesh. However the berries, leaves and flowers have been used in many past medicines. It also has long associations with May Day – its wood was used to make the first Maypoles.

DECIDUOUS

stiff with brown buds

CHAMPION TREE

HETHEL. NORFOLK
GIRTH 245 cm

deep red, oval-shaped fruits called haws

haws contain one seed each, unlike those of the Midland hawthorn, which contain two

long thorns up to 1.5 cm long

dark green

HEIGHT 12–15 m

WHERE Widespread; hedgerows, shrubland

FLOWERING May/June

FRUITING March/April

LEAF TINT/FALL November

OTHER NAMES May, whitethorn, quickthorn, tramp's supper, holy innocents

USES Walking sticks, tool handles

small, white, flowers grow in clusters after the leaves have appeared

three to seven deep lobes

MY OBSERVATIONS

Season: _____

Where is the tree? _____

_____

Describe the tree: _____

_____

What wildlife can you see? _____

_____

How tall is your tree? _____

_____

Honey bees visit flowers, such as those of horse chestnut, for nectar. They also carry pollen on their bodies to other flowers. This helps fertilise the flowers so that they will produce seeds.

SEEN IT?

MEASURED IT?

MY DRAWINGS AND PHOTOS

On my tree I saw: leaves ○   buds ○   fruit ○   flowers ○

Horse chestnut *Aesculus hippocastanum*

Horse chestnuts are best known for their glossy, brown nuts known as conkers. Competitors meet up in Northamptonshire every year to battle in the World Conker Championships – an event that has been running since 1965. Horse chestnut trees arrived in Britain in the 16th century and possibly get their name from the practice of feeding conkers to horses to cure them of illness.

DECIDUOUS

flowers have five petals and a small pink spot near the centre

sticky buds

upright spikes of white flowers

HEIGHT 14–28 m

WHERE Widespread; woodland, parks, hedgerows

FLOWERING May

FRUITING September/October

LEAF TINT/FALL October/November

OTHER NAMES Conker tree

USES Extract from nuts is used to make herbal medicines

five to seven long leaflets appear in early spring

about 6 cm wide

one brown nut, (conker), inside each spiky green fruit

leaflets fan out and are on a sturdy stalk

MY OBSERVATIONS

Season: _____

Where is the tree? _____

_____

Describe the tree: _____

_____

_____

What wildlife can you see? _____

_____

_____

How tall is your tree? _____

_____

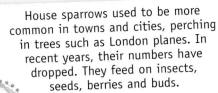

House sparrows used to be more common in towns and cities, perching in trees such as London planes. In recent years, their numbers have dropped. They feed on insects, seeds, berries and buds.

SEEN IT?

MEASURED IT?

MY DRAWINGS AND PHOTOS

On my tree I saw: leaves ○   buds ○   fruit ○   flowers ○

HAND-
SHAPED

London plane trees are a familiar sight in many cities and towns. They were widely planted along streets in urban areas because they tolerate pollution. In the 17th century, American plane and oriental plane trees were cross-bred to produce this new variety. The London plane sheds dirt in it's bark, which peels off through the year revealing a paler yellow bark beneath. Its attractive, hard-wearing timber is also known as 'lacewood'.

DECIDUOUS

HEIGHT 13–35 m

WHERE Widespread; streets, parks, cities, towns

FLOWERING May/June

FRUITING September/October

LEAF TINT/FALL October/ November

OTHER NAMES Hybrid plane

USES Furniture

green with smooth, pink buds

male flowers are round and yellow

female flowers are round and reddish

lobes have triangular tips

up to 25 cm long

each spiky fruit contains many seeds

many fruit cases stay on the tree throughout the winter

MY OBSERVATIONS

Season: _____

Where is the tree? _____

_____

Describe the tree: _____

_____

_____

What wildlife can you see? _____

_____

_____

How tall is your tree? _____

_____

SEEN IT?

MEASURED IT?

In winter, the large, oval outline of a tawny owl may be seen against the branches of a sycamore tree. Owls have brilliant eyesight and hearing.

MY DRAWINGS AND PHOTOS

On my tree I saw: leaves ○   buds ○   fruit ○   flowers ○

Sycamore *Acer pseudoplatanus*

I n the autumn, sycamores produce thousands of spinning, winged fruits called 'keys'. The wings act like helicopter blades and spin the keys through the air so that they land a distance from the tree. The sycamore is also known as the martyrs' tree. In England in 1834, a group of workers – the Tolpuddle Martyrs – met under a sycamore to form a society to fight for better wages. They were expelled from the country as punishment.

DECIDUOUS

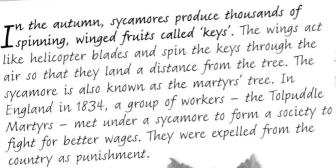

each individual flower has five petals

yellow-green flowers hang in spikes

winged fruits, or keys, are green at first, then ripen to brown

up to 15 cm long with five lobes

green buds grow in opposite pairs

each key holds two seeds

HEIGHT 16–35 m

WHERE Widespread; woodland, hedgerows, mountains

FLOWERING April/May

FRUITING September

LEAF TINT/FALL October/November

OTHER NAMES Great maple, great plane, martyrs' tree

USES Furniture, veneers, musical instruments

CHAMPION TREE
BIRNAM, PERTH & KINROSS
GIRTH 723 cm

stalks are often red

insects ○ birds ○ mammals ○ fungi ○ other . . . .

MY OBSERVATIONS

Season: _____

Where is the tree? _____

_____

Describe the tree: _____

_____

_____

What wildlife can you see? _____

_____

_____

How tall is your tree? _____

_____

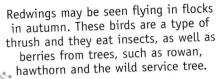

Redwings may be seen flying in flocks in autumn. These birds are a type of thrush and they eat insects, as well as berries from trees, such as rowan, hawthorn and the wild service tree.

SEEN IT?

MEASURED IT?

MY DRAWINGS AND PHOTOS

On my tree I saw: leaves ○   buds ○   fruit ○   flowers ○

Wild service tree *Sorbus torminalis*

The wild service tree is an indicator of ancient woodland – areas where there has been continuous woodland since at least 1600. In spring, white blossom covers this tree and in autumn, its leaves turn copper-red. Its berries, which were used to cure stomach upsets until the 1700s, are best eaten when overripe. This tree also goes by the name of 'chequers'. Some say this refers to the bark peeling off in squares and leaving a chequerboard effect.

DECIDUOUS

HEIGHT 10–25 m

WHERE Southern England, Wales; ancient woodland

FLOWERING May/June

FRUITING September–November

LEAF TINT/FALL October/November

OTHER NAMES Chequers

USES Fruits used to make an alcoholic drink called 'Chequers'

stalks are hairy

green buds

reddish-brown, berry-like fruits

small white flowers hang in clusters on stalks

slightly glossy on upper surface

up to 10 cm long

MY OBSERVATIONS

Season: _____

Where is the tree? _____

_____

Describe the tree: _____

_____

_____

What wildlife can you see? _____

_____

_____

How tall is your tree? _____

_____

King Alfred's cake fungus is also called coal fungus. It is ball-shaped and dark in colour. It grows on fallen trees, especially ash and beech. Dried fungus makes good tinder for fires.

SEEN IT?

MEASURED IT?

MY DRAWINGS AND PHOTOS

On my tree I saw: leaves ○   buds ○   fruit ○   flowers ○

Ash Fraxinus excelsior

The stately ash is one of the tallest deciduous trees in Europe and it grows easily in many habitats across Britain. In Scandinavian mythology, the ash was regarded as the tree of life. In English folklore, it was used to predict the weather. If oak buds opened before ash buds then the summer would be dry, but if ash buds opened first, the summer would be wet. Like many trees, the ash was once believed to provide defence against black magic and witchcraft.

DECIDUOUS

HEIGHT 15–30 m

WHERE Widespread; woodland, hedgerows, hillsides

FLOWERING April

FRUITING June

LEAF TINT/FALL September/ October

OTHER NAMES Lofty ash, fuinnseog (Irish)

USES Oars, farm tools, spade handles

black buds

purplish clusters of petalless flowers

flowers appear before leaves

some keys stay on the tree through winter, after the leaves have fallen

toothed edges

winged fruits, called ash keys, hang in clusters

three to six pairs of leaflets with a single leaflet at the top

CHAMPION TREE
MOCCAS PARK,
HEREFORDSHIRE
GIRTH 825 cm

insects ○ birds ○ mammals ○ fungi ○ other . . . .

MY OBSERVATIONS

Season:

Where is the tree?

Describe the tree:

What wildlife can you see?

How tall is your tree?

SEEN IT?

MEASURED IT?

Jelly ear fungus is a rubbery, ear-shaped fungus that is dark in colour. It often grows on dead elder and elm trees and is best seen in winter and spring. Each lobe can grow up to 10 cm across.

MY DRAWINGS AND PHOTOS

On my tree I saw: leaves ○   buds ○   fruit ○   flowers ○

Elder *Sambucus nigra*

The elder has proved to be a useful British tree, with the flowers, berries and stems all being put to good use. 'Elder' comes from the Anglo Saxon word 'aeld', meaning 'fire'. The stems are hollow and were once used to blow air into fires. In Denmark, the tree was associated with magic and, before a tree could be cut down, permission had to be sought from its spirit. The flowers can be made into a cordial and the berries into wine.

DECIDUOUS

soft and white in centre

pale flowers have a sickly fragrance

Each tiny flower has three to five petals

each stalk has two to four pairs of small leaflets with a single one at the tip

small, shiny, black berries on red stalks

heavy clusters hang downwards

oval leaflets

HEIGHT Up to 10 m
WHERE Widespread; hedgerows, scrubland
FLOWERING June/July
FRUITING August/September
LEAF TINT/FALL October/November
OTHER NAMES Elderflower, common elder, black elder
USES Toys, wooden spoons

insects ○ birds ○ mammals ○ fungi ○ other . . . .

MY OBSERVATIONS

Season: _____

Where is the tree? _____

_____

Describe the tree: _____

_____

_____

What wildlife can you see? _____

_____

_____

How tall is your tree? _____

_____

SEEN IT?

MEASURED IT?

The buff-tip moth avoids predators by resting on a stem to look like a broken twig. The yellow-black larvae of this moth feeds on the leaves of deciduous trees, including laburnum.

MY DRAWINGS AND PHOTOS

On my tree I saw: leaves ○   buds ○   fruit ○   flowers ○

Laburnum — *Laburnum anagyroides*

A common sight in British gardens, laburnum is recognisable by its cascades of bright yellow flowers in the summer. It originated in Europe and was introduced to Britain in the 16th century. All parts of the tree are poisonous, especially the seeds. The heartwood is deep brown in colour and was highly prized for making decorative items. It was often used as a substitute for the dark wood of the tropical ebony tree.

DECIDUOUS

HEIGHT 6–9 m

WHERE Widespread; parks, gardens

FLOWERING May/June

FRUITING September/October

LEAF TINT/FALL October–December

OTHER NAMES Goldenchain, goldenrain

USES Grown for ornament

grey-green, with soft hairs when young

long spikes covered in many yellow flowers

each hanging cluster of flowers is called a raceme

seed pods dry and open while still on the tree

each leaf is made up of three oval leaflets

seed pods release black seeds that are very poisonous

MY OBSERVATIONS

Season: _____

Where is the tree? _____

_____

Describe the tree: _____

_____

_____

What wildlife can you see? _____

_____

_____

How tall is your tree? _____

_____

SEEN IT?

MEASURED IT?

The rowan tree's ripening red berries provide a feast for many birds, such as the mistle thrush. They visit berry-laden trees in winter, and will often defend a tree from other birds.

MY DRAWINGS AND PHOTOS

On my tree I saw: leaves ○   buds ○   fruit ○   flowers ○

Rowan *Sorbus aucuparia*

The magical rowan tree has a past steeped in history and mythology. 'Rowan' comes from the old Norse word for tree – 'raun'. Its wood was used by druids to make staffs and wands. People used to put sprigs of rowan in their houses to protect them from lightning, and sailors took it on board boats to protect them from storms. Raw berries are poisonous, but once cooked they can be eaten. As well as food and drink, they have been used in herbal medicines.

DECIDUOUS

purple-brown buds are covered in grey hairs

orange-red berries up to 1 cm long

HEIGHT 8–15 m

WHERE Widespread; mountains, parks, gardens

FLOWERING May

FRUITING October/November

LEAF TINT/FALL October/November

OTHER NAMES Mountain ash, whispering tree, witchbane

USES Bows, tool handles, bowls

small, cream-coloured flowers grow in dense clusters

each fruit contains one or two seeds

five to eight pairs of leaflets

orange and reddish-brown in autumn

CHAMPION TREE

COTHERSTONE, DURHAM
GIRTH 340 cm

MY OBSERVATIONS

Season: _____

Where is the tree? _____

_____

Describe the tree: _____

_____

What wildlife can you see? _____

_____

How tall is your tree? _____

MEASURED IT?

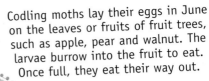

Codling moths lay their eggs in June on the leaves or fruits of fruit trees, such as apple, pear and walnut. The larvae burrow into the fruit to eat. Once full, they eat their way out.

SEEN IT?

MY DRAWINGS AND PHOTOS

On my tree I saw: leaves ○   buds ○   fruit ○   flowers ○

Walnut *Juglans regia*

Walnut trees have been grown in Britain for their nuts, but also for their timber, which is one of the most beautiful woods in the world. There is evidence that walnuts have been growing in Britain since at least Roman times, and they were widely planted in the 1800s. Thousands of walnut trees were felled in the Napoleonic wars so that the timber could be used to make guns for soldiers.

DECIDUOUS

male catkins grow up to 15 cm long

female flowers are small and green

fruits are round and green

an edible nut is inside the tough outer casing

thick with a leathery surface

hollow inside

five to nine leaflets

HEIGHT 10–30 m

WHERE Southern England; woodland, parks

FLOWERING April–June

FRUITING September/October

LEAF TINT/FALL October/November

OTHER NAMES Persian walnut, common walnut

USES Furniture, veneers, nuts eaten as food

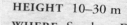

insects ○ birds ○ mammals ○ fungi ○ other . . . .

MY OBSERVATIONS

Season:
_____

Where is the tree?
_____

_____

Describe the tree:
_____

_____

What wildlife can you see?
_____

_____

How tall is your tree?
_____

SEEN IT?

MEASURED IT?

Starlings are noisy, colourful birds that flock around tall trees, such as cedars. They nest in tree cavities, and often hop around the ground near tree roots searching for ants and other bugs.

MY DRAWINGS AND PHOTOS

On my tree I saw: leaves O   buds O   fruit O   flowers O

Cedar of Lebanon *Cedrus libani*

This cedar is native to the mountain forests of the eastern Mediterranean, and has been a popular tree to plant in parkland and large gardens in the UK. In ancient times, many of the cedar forests in Lebanon were felled to supply timber for building materials and fuel. Some stories tell of how it was first brought to Europe in the 18th century by a Frenchman, who uprooted a seedling while travelling in the Middle East. Not having a flowerpot he stored the young tree in his hat, looking after it until his return to Paris.

EVERGREEN

HEIGHT 8–35 m

WHERE Widespread; parks, large gardens, churchyards

FLOWERING June–September

FRUITING August–October

LEAF TINT/FALL Evergreen

OTHER NAMES Lebanese cedar

USES Buildings, furniture

seed cones ripen to brown

up to 15 cm long

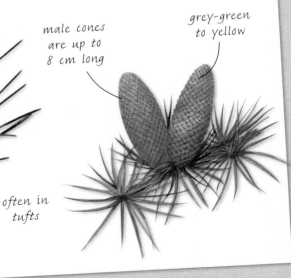

male cones are up to 8 cm long

grey-green to yellow

often in tufts

needles are up to 3 cm long

insects ○ birds ○ mammals ○ fungi ○ other . . . .

MY OBSERVATIONS

Season: _____

Where is the tree? _____

_____

Describe the tree: _____

_____

_____

What wildlife can you see? _____

_____

_____

How tall is your tree? _____

_____

SEEN IT?

MEASURED IT?

The common crossbill belongs to the finch family, and is often found near conifers, such as larches, as they eat the seeds. Crossbills make their nests out of twigs, moss, wool and hair.

MY DRAWINGS AND PHOTOS

On my tree I saw: leaves ○   buds ○   fruit ○   flowers ○

European larch *Larix decidua*

Larches grow tall and straight and, unusually for conifers, they lose their leaves in the autumn. These fast-growing trees produce good quality timber and they are often seen growing in plantations. In Siberia, it was once believed that man was created from a larch tree, and that woman was created separately from a conifer or fir tree. Herbalists use a weak tea made from the inner bark to treat stomach upsets and asthma.

DECIDUOUS

HEIGHT 12–30 m

WHERE Widespread; woodland, parks, gardens, plantations

FLOWERING March/April

FRUITING September

LEAF TINT/FALL October/November

OTHER NAMES Common larch

USES Fences, furniture, boat-building

seed cones open to release seeds

female flower is pink-red

young needles

male flowers are soft, yellow cones

reddish brown bark

needles grow in bunches

up to 3 cm in length

MY OBSERVATIONS

Season: _____

Where is the tree? _____

_____

Describe the tree: _____

_____

_____

What wildlife can you see? _____

_____

_____

How tall is your tree? _____

_____

SEEN IT?

MEASURED IT?

Treecreepers have long toes that allow them to hang upside down and scuttle quickly up a tree. They have brown-and-white mottled feathers, and are known to roost in sequoia trunks.

MY DRAWINGS AND PHOTOS

On my tree I saw: leaves ○   buds ○   fruit ○   flowers ○

Giant sequoia *Sequioadendron giganteum*

The giant sequoia is one of the tallest-growing plants in the world and is also one of the longest living, capable of surviving up to 4000 years. The tallest specimen is the General Sherman in the United States, which, in 1987, measured 83.8 m tall. Giant sequoias come from California and were brought to Britain in 1853, the year that the Duke of Wellington died. This is how this tree got its other name – Wellingtonia. The yew is one of few trees known to survive to a similar age.

EVERGREEN

HEIGHT 20–50 m

WHERE Widespread; parks, grounds of historic buildings

FLOWERING May/June

FRUITING All year

LEAF TINT/FALL Evergreen

OTHER NAMES Mammoth tree, Wellingtonia

USES Leaves used in wreaths, and floral displays

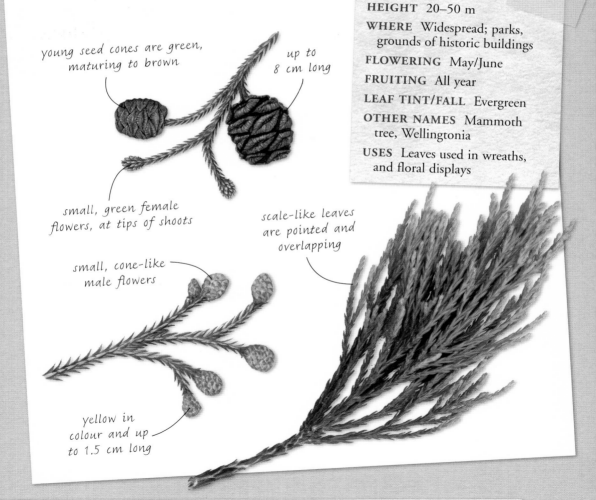

young seed cones are green, maturing to brown

up to 8 cm long

small, green female flowers, at tips of shoots

scale-like leaves are pointed and overlapping

small, cone-like male flowers

yellow in colour and up to 1.5 cm long

insects ○ birds ○ mammals ○ fungi ○ other . . . .

MY OBSERVATIONS

Season: _____

Where is the tree? _____

_____

Describe the tree: _____

_____

_____

What wildlife can you see? _____

_____

_____

How tall is your tree? _____

_____

SEEN IT?

MEASURED IT?

The juniper carpet moth feeds mainly on juniper trees. These insects are only found in a few places in Britain and they are very well camouflaged. They fly from October to November.

MY DRAWINGS AND PHOTOS

On my tree I saw: leaves ○   buds ○   fruit ○   flowers ○

Juniper *Juniperus communis*

Juniper is a small, slow-growing, evergreen tree and can be found in a wide range of habitats all around the world. Its fruits can take two to three years to ripen, so you may see black and green berries on the same tree. These are actually soft cones rather than true berries. As birds eat them and fly to other trees, they help distribute the seeds. In folklore, in parts of southwest England, the wood and needles were burned near a sick person — this was thought to cure infection.

EVERGREEN

male flowers are small, yellow cones

shoots are covered in slender, pointed needles

HEIGHT 5–10 m

WHERE Mainly southern England; woodland, scrubland, chalky soils

FLOWERING May/June

FRUITING All year

LEAF TINT/FALL Evergreen

OTHER NAMES Common juniper, dwarf juniper

USES Wood used to smoke meat, fruits used to flavour gin

up to 8 mm long

berry-like fruits take two to three years to ripen to black

needles grow in groups, or whorls, of three

female flowers are tiny, green, scaly cones

MY OBSERVATIONS

Season: _____

Where is the tree? _____

_____

Describe the tree: _____

_____

_____

What wildlife can you see? _____

_____

_____

How tall is your tree? _____

_____

Coal tits are often seen near Norway spruces and other conifer trees. These tiny birds form large flocks in autumn and winter, in search of food, such as insects and seeds.

SEEN IT?

MEASURED IT?

MY DRAWINGS AND PHOTOS

On my tree I saw: leaves ○   buds ○   fruit ○   flowers ○

Norway spruce *Picea abies*

It is believed that the Norway spruce was growing in Britain long before the last Ice Age. This species did not return to Britain until around the 1500s when it was brought over from Europe. It is grown in plantations for timber and also for use as Christmas trees. The German tradition of decorating Christmas trees became fashionable in England in the 19th century after Queen Victoria married the German nobleman, Prince Albert.

EVERGREEN

HEIGHT 18–40 m

WHERE Widespread; plantations parks

FLOWERING May

FRUITING September–November

LEAF TINT/FALL Evergreen

OTHER NAMES Spruce fir

USES Timber, paper, Christmas trees

short, stiff needles grow in a spiral pattern

rough and scaly

reddish male cones turn yellow when pollen is produced

small male cones grow close to the end of shoots

female flowers are reddish-brown and darken with age

mature seed cones are up to 17 cm long and hold many small seeds

insects ○ birds ○ mammals ○ fungi ○ other . . . .

MY OBSERVATIONS

Season: _____

Where is the tree? _____

_____

Describe the tree: _____

_____

_____

What wildlife can you see? _____

_____

_____

How tall is your tree? _____

_____

SEEN IT?

MEASURED IT?

Wood ants live in colonies of up to half a million individuals. Some make their nests by piling up pine needles and other plant matter. They are reddish-brown in colour and up to 1 cm long.

MY DRAWINGS AND PHOTOS

On my tree I saw: leaves ○   buds ○   fruit ○   flowers ○

Scots pine *Pinus sylvestris*

There are many conifers growing in Britain today, but the Scots pine is native to parts of Scotland, making it the only native British pine. These fast-growing trees are found from Spain to Siberia. Scots pine trees grow tall and straight, and the wood is very hard-wearing, which makes it ideal for use as telegraph poles. Long ago, the wood was used in ship-making and for water pipes. The cones have been used to forecast weather — it is thought that when the cones open the air is dry, so no rain should be expected.

EVERGREEN

CHAMPION TREE
MUIRWARD WOOD,
PERTH & KINROSS
GIRTH 628 cm

long, slender needles up to 8 cm long

small, yellow male cones grow in groups

HEIGHT 12–36 m

WHERE Widespread; woodland, plantations

FLOWERING April

FRUITING April

LEAF TINT/FALL Evergreen

OTHER NAMES Scots fir, giuis (Irish)

USES Fences, flooring, telegraph poles, railway sleepers

red female flowers grow in pairs

seed cones are green at first, taking two years to ripen

needles grow in pairs

mature seed cones are woody and up to 7 cm long

MY OBSERVATIONS

Season: _____

Where is the tree? _____

_____

Describe the tree: _____

_____

_____

What wildlife can you see? _____

_____

_____

How tall is your tree? _____

_____

Nuthatches are small birds with strong feet and ultra-sharp claws, and they are able to run head first down a tree trunk. They are one of many birds that may be seen in yew trees eating the fruits.

SEEN IT?

MEASURED IT?

MY DRAWINGS AND PHOTOS

On my tree I saw: leaves O   buds O   fruit O   flowers O

Yew *Taxus baccata*

The dark, mysterious yew tree has been the subject of myths and legends for centuries, and it can often be found in cemeteries and church grounds. Known to live for hundreds – sometimes thousands – of years, several churchyard yews are more than 1000 years old. In ancient times, people planted yews where they would be buried. Most parts of a yew tree are extremely poisonous to humans and animals.

EVERGREEN

HEIGHT 4–20 m

WHERE Widespread; churchyards, woodland

FLOWERING March/April

FRUITING October

LEAF TINT/FALL Evergreen

OTHER NAMES Iur (Irish)

USES Furniture, tool handles, an anti-cancer drug is made from the leaves

male flowers sit at the bases of leaves

needle-like leaves

small yellow flowers turn yellow when they release pollen

narrow, flat and dark green

fruits are red, berry-like fruits, called arils

female flowers are tiny, green cones 1 to 2 mm long

CHAMPION TREE
ULCOMBE PARISH CHURCH,
KENT
GIRTH 990 cm

insects ○ birds ○ mammals ○ fungi ○ other . . . .